## English words that come from Indonesian

gecko
ketchup
sarong
bamboo
cockatoo
mango
orang-utan

# Welcome to Indonesia

Meredith Costain   Paul Collins

This edition first published in 2002 in the United States of America by Chelsea House Publishers, a subsidiary of Haights Cross Communications



Chelsea House Publishers
1974 Sproul Road, Suite 400
Broomall, PA 19008–0914

The Chelsea House world wide web address is www.chelseahouse.com.

Library of Congress Cataloging-in-Publication Data Applied for.
ISBN 0-7910-6543-X

First published in 2000 by
Macmillan Education Australia Pty Ltd
627 Chapel Street, South Yarra, Australia, 3141





Edited by Miriana Dasovic
Text design and page layout by Goanna Graphics (Vic) Pty Ltd
Cover design by Goanna Graphics (Vic) Pty Ltd
Maps by Stephen Pascoe
Illustrations by Vaughan Duck
Printed in Hong Kong

**Acknowledgements**
The author and the publisher are grateful to the following for permission to reproduce copyright material:

Cover photograph: Children playing in the sea, Great Southern Stock © Jim Hooper.

Sandra Gago pp. 5–7, 13, 30; Great Southern Stock, pp. 14, 19 (bottom) © Greg Elms, pp. 9, 12, 18, 21 (bottom), 24 (top), 27 (bottom) © Jim Hooper, pp. 15 (right), 25 © Richard I'Anson, p. 23 (bottom) © Brian Wilkes; Blaine Harrington pp. 8, 10, 11 (right), 15 (left), 19 (top), 21 (top), 24 (bottom), 26, 27 (top), 28; Lonely Planet Images, pp. 22, 29 © Bernard Napthine; Sabine Schulte pp. 11 (left), 20, 23 (top), 30.

While every care has been taken to trace and acknowledge copyright the publishers tender their apologies for any accidental infringement where copyright has proved untraceable.

# Contents

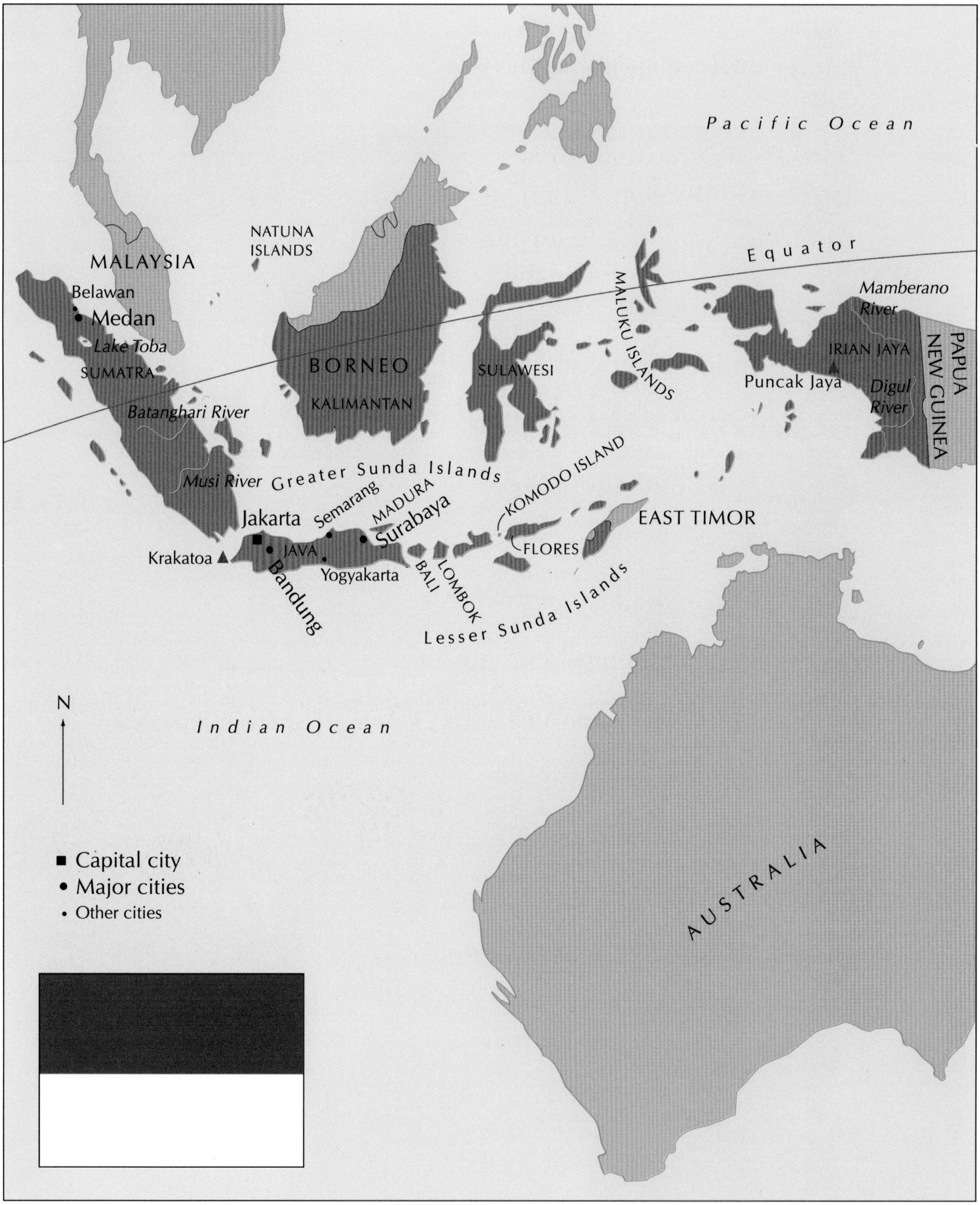

Pacific Ocean
MALAYSIA
NATUNA ISLANDS
Belawan
Medan
Lake Toba
SUMATRA
Batanghari River
Musi River
BORNEO
KALIMANTAN
SULAWESI
MALUKU ISLANDS
Equator
Mamberano River
IRIAN JAYA
Puncak Jaya
Digul River
PAPUA NEW GUINEA
Greater Sunda Islands
KOMODO ISLAND
Jakarta
Semarang
MADURA
Surabaya
EAST TIMOR
Krakatoa
JAVA
Bandung
Yogyakarta
BALI
LOMBOK
FLORES
Lesser Sunda Islands
N
Indian Ocean
AUSTRALIA

■ Capital city
• Major cities
• Other cities

# Welcome to Indonesia! Hi!

*Halo!* My name is Nining. I live in a village near Lovina Beach. It is on the north coast of Bali, which is one of Indonesia's many islands.

Indonesia has more islands than any other country in the world. A chain of over 17,000 islands stretches between the Pacific and Indian Oceans for almost 5,000 kilometers (3,107 miles). Only about 3,000 of the islands have people living on them. Our capital, Jakarta, is on Java. Other islands include Sulawesi, Sumatra, Lombok and Flores.

Kalimantan, which is part of the island of Borneo, and Irian Jaya, the western part of the island of New Guinea, also belong to Indonesia. Our nearest neighbors are Papua New Guinea, Australia and Malaysia. There are 300 different groups of people living in our country. Each group has its own culture and way of speaking. Many people also speak our official language, Bahasa Indonesia. Our national motto, 'Unity through diversity', makes a lot of sense!

Our flag is red and white. The red stripe stands for courage, and the white stripe for purity. It became our official emblem after **World War 2**.

# Family life

My family lives in a *kampung* called Bunut Panggang. A *kampung* is like a self-contained village. It contains our school, our mosque, and *warungs* selling groceries and lollies. Everything we need is here. Our *kampung* is bordered by the beach on one side, and the main road on the other. There are no roads inside our village, but there are lots of dogs and chickens!

I have a brother, Walit, who is 12, and a baby brother called Sultan. My cousins Aziz and Randi live next door. We all play together every afternoon. My favorite games are hopscotch and knucklebones, which is a throwing game played with bones. Sometimes we go swimming in the cold springs near the beach.

*My brothers, my cousins and me on my father's new Honda. You often see whole families packed onto motorbikes.*

*My grandparents,* **kakek** *and* **nenek***, live next door. For many years,* kakek *was a fisherman. Now he stays at home in the* kampung *and chats with his friends about his trips to sea.*

My father, Anwar, is a primary school teacher. Luckily, I am not in his class. My friends tell me he is very strict! My mother, Makmu, works at home. There is always plenty to do. When I am older, I will help her around the house. For now, she lets me play all day.

*This is our kitchen. Every morning my mother lights a fire in the brick stove so she can cook a big pot of rice. She also uses the kerosene cooker to stir-fry noodles and fry bananas. She makes enough food to last the whole day.*

# School

Indonesian children start school at the age of seven, but many children first spend two years in kindergarten. They must attend school until they are 12. After that, they can choose whether they want to go on to secondary school or not. However, many families cannot afford to keep their children at school. They stay home to help their parents instead.

There are six grades in primary school. These are followed by three years of middle school, and then three years of high school. After high school, some students go on to universities or technical colleges.

My school day starts at 7:00 a.m. and finishes at 12:30 p.m. Our teacher is very strict. No one would ever dream of playing up in class! After school we go home for lunch, then play for the rest of the day. My subjects include Balinese, Bahasa Indonesia, religion, maths, art, singing and dancing. I like singing best!

*Schoolchildren near Ubud, in Bali. Children like to walk to school in a big group with their friends and brothers and sisters.*

# Sports and leisure

Our most popular sports are soccer, volleyball, tennis, badminton and ping-pong. Our professional volleyball and badminton players are doing very well. In 1997, Heryanto Arbiis became the world badminton champion.

On the island of Madura, near Java, bulls are bred for racing. The driver stands or sits on a wooden **yoke** fixed between two bulls. The bulls run very fast. The driver has to hang on for his life! Many other regions include bull-racing in their festivals. In West Sumatra, they hold duck races!

We also practice our own form of martial arts. One style is similar to kung fu. It is called *Silat Gerak Pilihan*, or *SiGePi*. Peasants originally used it to defend themselves against attacks by their landlords! Blows are only allowed to the chest or stomach. Weapons such as the *toya*, a staff, and *golok*, a machete, are used in fights.

*Rubber tires make good toys, especially when you live close to the sea!*

# Indonesian culture

Music and dancing play a big part in our culture. You will find *gamelan* orchestras playing all over Java and Bali. At night, the drums and gongs can be heard from miles away. Some *gamelan* orchestras have over 50 different instruments. These include bamboo flutes, metal and wooden gongs, goatskin drums and stringed instruments.

Each of our dances tells a story. It might be about warriors preparing for battle, or about a battle between good and evil. The good guy always wins in our dances! In the *kechak*, or monkey dance, Prince Rama joins forces with the king of monkeys to help save his kidnapped wife. The monkey dancers make a chattering sound as they dance. It sounds like '*kechak – kechak – kechak – kechak*'!

*A children's* gamelan *orchestra plays at Peliatan in Bali.* Gamelan *orchestras play for many of our dances. We also use them at festivals, religious ceremonies and shadow puppet shows.*

*The Balinese* legong *dance is performed by young girls in tightly bound costumes, decorated with gold.*

*A **batik** artist at work. Designs are dotted onto silk or cotton with a fine 'pen' containing wax. The material is then dipped into dye. The first lot of wax is scraped off, and a new design dotted on. The material is then dipped and waxed and dipped again until the design is finished.*

Shadow puppet plays, performed behind a screen, are also used to tell stories. The puppeteers, called *dalangs*, are highly skilled. They train for eight years and practice daily. A *dalang* works all the puppets himself, using both his hands. He also has to create all the voices for the different puppets. Some shows have as many as 100 puppets and last nearly the whole night!

# Festivals and religion

Most of the festivals in Indonesia are tied to our religion. Over 90 percent of Indonesians are Muslim. Every year we celebrate *Idul Fitri*. It is held at the end of **Ramadan**, which is a time of fasting. *Idul Fitri* is a time of feasting! All the women in my *kampung* spend the last week of Ramadan cooking thousands of biscuits on top of their tiny kerosene stoves. The next day, which is the first day of *Idul Fitri*, they put the biscuits out for visitors to eat.

Although my family is Muslim, most people living in Bali are Hindu. Bali has many thousands of temples containing statues of the hundreds of Hindu gods and goddesses. Each day, people leave offerings of flowers and fruit at the temples. The legends of kings and gods are told through Balinese dances.

*A Balinese temple procession. Temple festivals are held each year to chase demons, or to honor special objects such as daggers or household tools.*

*A group of Muslim girls chant from the Koran, the sacred book of Islam, at a wedding ceremony.*

| **Indonesian Holidays** | |
|---|---|
| New Year's Day | January 1 |
| *Nyepi* | March |
| Easter | March/April |
| Independence Day | August 17 |
| Armed Forces Day | October 5 |
| Christmas Day | December 25 |

Many of the people living in northern Sumatra and north Sulawesi are Christian. They were converted by missionaries in the 1700s. Some of the people living in the distant islands still follow the old religions of our country. They believe that spirits are found in all living things. Trees, animals, and natural forces such as the wind, all contain spiritual beings.

*Every year, the people from my* kampung *hold the* Sapi Gerumbungan, *or Cow-bells Festival. They compete to see whose team of bulls can plough a rice paddy in the fastest time. Points are also given for style. The bulls have to hold their heads up at a nice angle, and keep all their bells ringing while they work!*

# Food and shopping

In western Indonesia, rice is the most important ingredient in cooking. Two quick and tasty meals are *nasi goreng,* which is fried rice with eggs, chicken and vegetables, and *mie goreng,* which is a spicy noodle and vegetable dish. In other parts of Indonesia, sago, yams, or sweet potato form the main part of meals.

*A* warung *filled with delicious dishes.* Warungs *are the Indonesian version of fast-food outlets! Popular choices are* murtabak, *a sort of pancake, and satay, which is meat grilled on a skewer and served with peanut sauce.*

Sumatran food is hot and spicy. Pieces of fish and meat are often wrapped in banana and palm leaves before they are cooked. Roast suckling pig, known as *babi guling,* is made for special occasions in Bali. However, my family does not eat pork because we are Muslim.

My mother gets up early and cooks enough rice, vegetables and fried bananas to last our family the whole day. She puts the food under special covers to keep the flies away. When we get hungry, we grab some food from under the covers to nibble on. We rarely sit down and have a meal together, as it is not part of our culture to do so. Sometimes we use a spoon or fork to eat our meal, but mostly we use just our fingers. We always eat with our right hand. This is another Muslim tradition.

*There are many interesting types of fruit in Indonesia. We have breadfruit, rambutans, papayas, jack fruit, mangoes and pineapples. My favorite fruit is the durian. It smells disgusting, but tastes delicious!*

*A floating market in Kalimantan. Most shopping in Indonesia is done either at markets or small roadside stalls.*

# Make chicken satay

The peanut sauce served with satay is delicious! You can also serve it with *gado gado*. This is a salad made with hard-boiled eggs and lightly steamed vegetables such as beans, carrots and potatoes.

## Ask an adult to help you prepare this dish.

### You will need:

**For the satays**

- 500 grams (1 lb) chicken fillet or thighs, without skin
- oil
- chunks of pineapple and cucumber for serving

**For the peanut sauce**

- 6 tablespoons crunchy peanut butter
- 2/3 cup water
- 2 tablespoons dark soy sauce
- 1 tablespoon lemon juice
- 2 tablespoons coconut milk
- 1/2 teaspoon chili powder
- 1 teaspoon ground coriander

### What to do:

1. Cut the chicken into cubes. Push them onto skewers.
2. Brush the cubes lightly with oil. Grill or barbecue them until cooked, usually about eight minutes.
3. Put the peanut butter and the water into a saucepan. Stir over gentle heat until well blended.
4. Stir in the rest of the ingredients. Add a little more water if needed to make a smooth paste.
5. Put the satays on a plate, along with the pineapple and cucumber chunks. Pour peanut sauce over the satays. Enjoy!

# Make shadow puppets

Indonesian shadow puppet shows are called *wayan kulit.* The puppet is held behind a screen. A light is shone onto the puppet from behind the screen. The audience, sitting in front of the screen, can see the puppet's shadow as it moves about.

## You will need:

- large pieces of colored card
- a pencil
- scissors
- tape
- canes or sticks
- a large screen
- a reading lamp

## What to do:

1 Draw some animals or people on the cards. Cut them out.

2 Tape the sticks to the back of the shadow puppets.

3 Stand behind the screen. Hold the puppets up. Ask a friend to shine the reading lamp onto your puppets from behind the screen. You should see their shadows showing through the front of the screen.

4 Act out your play. You will need to make all the noises or speak the puppets' parts yourself.

# Landscape and climate

Indonesia is a tropical wonderland made up of over 17,000 islands. There are four main groups of islands. They are the Greater Sunda islands, the Lesser Sunda islands, the Maluku islands, once known as the Moluccas or Spice Islands, and the islands around Irian Jaya. Many of the smaller islands are surrounded by coral reefs or divided by deep ocean trenches.

Most of our islands are covered by steep mountains. Our highest peak is Puncak Jaya, at 5,029 meters (16,500 feet). There are over 400 volcanoes in Indonesia. Many are still active. In 1883, the volcano on Krakatoa exploded. It was so violent that molten **lava** landed as far away as Madagascar, off the coast of Africa! Ash from volcanoes makes our soil very rich.

Indonesian rivers are short and fast-flowing. Our longest river is the Mamberamo, in Irian Jaya. Many beautiful lakes, such as Lake Toba in northern Sumatra, have formed in the craters of extinct volcanoes.

*A lake in a volcanic crater on the island of Flores.*

*Farmers cut terraces into steep slopes so that they will have enough land to grow rice.*

The **equator** runs through Indonesia. This means that our temperatures stay fairly even all year round. It is usually cooler in the mountains than by the coast, but the weather here is generally hot. Indonesia has only two seasons. The 'wet' season starts in November, when the rain-filled **monsoon** arrives from the Indian Ocean. The 'dry' season runs from May to October. It is the best time to visit our country.

## Average yearly temperatures

| | |
|---|---|
| Coastal plains | 28°C/82°F |
| Inland/mountain areas | 26°C/79°F |
| Higher mountain areas | 23°C/73°F |

*A boy from Sulawesi is drenched by the monsoon rains.*

# Plants and animals

Nearly two-thirds of Indonesia is covered with tropical **rainforests**. They contain thousands of different plants and animals, including 5,000 different types of orchid! Our rainforest timbers include *meranti*, sandalwood, ebony and teak. They are highly valued around the world. However, as more and more trees are cut down for export, many animals are losing their homes. Some animals, such as the Sumatran rhinoceros and the Javan tiger, are in danger of becoming **extinct**.

The *Rafflesia* grows in south-central Sumatra. It is the world's largest flower. The plant has five huge red and white petals, but no stem or leaves. It can grow to one meter (3 feet) wide and weigh as much as nine kilograms (20 pounds)! After blooming for a week, the flower withers away.

*The delicate flower of a waterlily.*

*Grey monkeys are found throughout Bali. Many grey monkeys live at ancient temple sites. They are often very cheeky, stealing cameras and hats from tourists!*

The orang-utan is found in the jungles of Sumatra and Kalimantan. The name means 'man of the forest'. Sulawesi is home to many strange creatures. They include the *babi rusa*, a deer-like pig, and the *anoa*, a dwarf buffalo. There is also an animal whose name, *binatang hantu*, means 'spooky animal'! Tree kangaroos are found on the islands of Maluku.

There are about 1,500 different types of birds in Indonesia, including cassowaries, birds of paradise, parrots, cockatoos and kingfishers. Giant sea turtles, crocodiles, sea horses and dolphins are found in the waters around our shores.

*The Komodo dragon is found on Komodo Island, east of Bali. It is the largest type of lizard in the world, and can grow up to four meters (13 feet) long.*

# Cities and landmarks

About one-third of the people of Indonesia live in towns or cities. Our capital city is Jakarta, on the island of Java. Jakarta is one of the largest cities in the world, with over nine million people. It is a mixture of the old and the new. There are shiny new office buildings and department stores, colonial-style houses built by the Dutch and Portuguese in the 1600s, and large areas of slums. Many houses are made of packing crates and sheets of tin, and have no toilets or running water. The streets of Jakarta are often clogged with traffic, and the air is full of smog.

Other large cities include Surabaya, a shipping and industrial center in east Java, and Medan, in northern Sumatra. Medan is home to one of the largest mosques in Indonesia. Motorbikes and jeeps crowd its roads, making it one of the noisiest cities in the world.

*Jakarta is a modern city, with wide streets and impressive monuments. It also has large areas of slums.*

Indonesia has many fine temples. Tanah Lot is built on a huge rock off the coast of Bali. Poisonous sea snakes live in the caves below the temple. They are thought to be holy guardians of the site. The Prambanan Temple in central Java has stone sculptures of many of the famous characters from ancient Hindu myths.

Goa Gajah, *the Elephant Cave, in Bali. It was carved out of rock by Buddhists more than 1,000 years ago. Inside the cave is a statue of Ganesa, the elephant-headed god of obstacles.*

*Borobudur is the largest Buddhist temple in the world. It was built 1,200 years ago near the city of Yogyakarta, in Java. Its many small shrines contain statues of Buddha.*

# Industry and agriculture

Indonesia is one of the world's largest producers of petroleum and tin. We have rich supplies of coal, nickel, iron ore and natural gas. The gas field in the Natuna Sea is the largest known source of natural gas in the world.

*An* ***ikat*** *weaver at her loom on the island of Flores. The yarn is dyed before it is woven. Sometimes gold and silver threads are woven into the borders of the cloth.*

*The rich soil around volcanic craters, such as Lake Batur in Bali, is ideal for growing crops.*

*Rice terraces near Ubud in Bali. Rice is our major crop.*

Our manufacturing industries have boomed over the last decade. Goods such as clothes and sports shoes are made in our many new factories. Next time you slip on a pair of Nikes, look for the 'Made In Indonesia' label under the tongue!

Many people work in the logging industry, cutting down rainforest hardwood trees. These will be felled to make timber for furniture, or pulped to make woodchips for paper. Every year our wood is exported to other countries. However, too many trees are being cut down without new ones being planted. Unless Indonesia changes this situation, we will soon lose one of our most valuable natural resources. The homes of many forest animals are also being destroyed by logging.

Two-thirds of our people work as farmers. We produce more rice than any other country in the world, but we still need to import rice to feed all our people. Other main crops include maize, sweet potatoes, peanuts, cassava and tropical fruit. Many people make their living by fishing.

# Transportation

It can be difficult to travel in Indonesia. There are thousands of islands, and many of our roads are in poor condition. The roads are often washed away by heavy rain. Sometimes whole bridges are swept away by floods.

*A motorbike is the fastest way to get around a big city like Jakarta.*

Few Indonesian people own cars. They rely on a variety of public transportation to travel within cities or from village to village. This includes minibuses, *bemos*, which are pick-up trucks with rows of seats along each side, and pedal-powered rickshaws called *becaks*. Many people ride bicycles.

Many of the islands are connected by a government shipping company. People also travel by private ferry or plane. Farmers often use the rivers to ferry their goods to the markets. Larger boats carry cars and other goods. Our main ports are Belawan, Jakarta and Surabaya.

*Villagers often carry local produce on their heads.*

*Boats are the best way to travel between our thousands of islands.*

# History and government

In 1890, people found fossils of 'Java Man' in east Java. The fossils were thought to be about 500,000 years old. This find dates back to **prehistoric times**! The first people to live in Indonesia were thought to have come from India or Burma, in mainland Asia. Later, around 3000 BC, new people from southern China arrived.

Since then, many people from many different nations have occupied our land. The Portuguese controlled most of the island trade in the 1500s. Christianity was introduced by Spanish and Portuguese traders in the 1600s. By the 1620s, the Dutch had started to control most of the islands. In 1641, they captured Malacca Island from the Portuguese. During the **Napoleonic Wars**, British forces took control of the country, which was then known as the Dutch East Indies.

*The Jakarta Historical Museum was once a building belonging to the Dutch East India Company. When the Dutch controlled the islands of Indonesia, Jakarta was known as Batavia.*

*The garuda appears on the Indonesian crest of arms. It is a fierce man-eagle. In Hindu mythology, garuda was ridden by the god Vishnu.*

By 1816, the Dutch had again taken control of Indonesia. Dutch rule finally ended in 1942, when Japanese forces occupied Indonesia during World War 2. The Japanese left in 1945, and Achmed Sukarno proclaimed Indonesia an independent **republic**. Sukarno became president in 1949. The Dutch tried to regain control once again, but finally recognized Indonesia's independence in 1949.

In 1975, the Portuguese suddenly left East Timor, and it was invaded by Indonesian forces. After a long struggle, East Timor finally became independent in 1999.

Today, Indonesia is divided into 27 administrative **provinces**. Each province is ruled by a governor who is appointed by the president. In recent times, Indonesia's government has been extremely unstable. There have been food shortages, riots and student protests in the streets. Our future is still uncertain.

# Fact file

**Official name**
Republic of Indonesia

**Population**
216,000,000

**Land area**
1,919,443 square kilometers (748,582 square miles)

**Government**
republic

**Language**
Bahasa Indonesia

**Religions**
Islam, Hinduism, Christianity, Buddhism

**Currency**
Rupiah (Rp)

**Capital city**
Jakarta

**Major cities**
Surabaya, Medan, Bandung, Semarang

**Number of islands**
17,508

**Climate**
Tropical, with hot and humid weather all year

**Major rivers**
Musi, Batanghari, Mamberamo, Digul

**Highest mountain**
Puncak Jaya 5,030 meters (16,503 feet)

**Main farm products**
rice, cassava, peanuts, rubber, cocoa, coffee, poultry, beef, pork

**Main industries**
petroleum, natural gas, textiles, clothing, mining, cement, chemical fertilizers, plywood, rubber, food, tourism

**Natural resources**
petroleum, tin, natural gas, nickel, timber, bauxite, copper, gold, silver

# Glossary

| | |
|---|---|
| **batik** | a method of printing on fabric using wax and dye |
| **equator** | an imaginary line around the earth that divides it into a northern and a southern half |
| **extinct** | when no more animals of this kind are left on earth |
| ***ikat*** | a traditional style of weaving, where the yarn is dyed before it is woven |
| ***kakek*** | grandpa |
| **lava** | molten rocks that erupt from a volcano |
| **monsoon** | a wind system that brings heavy rain |
| **Napoleonic Wars** | a series of European wars that lasted from 1803–1815 |
| ***nenek*** | grandma |
| **prehistoric times** | the time before history was written down, many hundreds of thousands of years ago |
| **province** | a large division or part of a country |
| **rainforests** | thick forests where rain falls almost every day |
| **Ramadan** | the ninth month of the Muslim year, when people fast during daylight hours |
| **republic** | a country that is ruled by an elected leader rather than a king, queen or emperor |
| ***warungs*** | street stalls |
| **World War 2** | a war from 1939 to 1945. The Allies (the United States, the Soviet Union, Britain, France and others) defeated the Axis powers (Germany, Italy and Japan) |
| **yoke** | a wooden frame that binds two animals, normally oxen, together by the neck |

# Index

one
two
dua
three
tiga
four
empat
five
lima
six
enam
seven
tujuh
eight
delapan
nine
sembilan
ten
sepuluh
hello
goodbye
selamat tinggal
please
tolong
thank you
terima kasih
terima kasih kembali
you're welcome
permisi
excuse me